Living Undiagnosed

A True Story

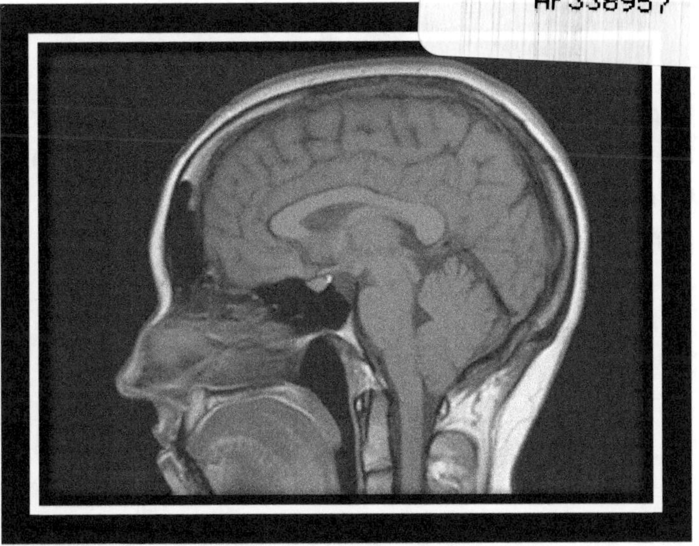

By Tania Stephanson

Contents

Introduction

Trapped; the only word I can use to explain the sensation of having an episode. It's like being inside a small, locked room surrounded by windows, searching for the doorknob to escape. Outside, life passes me by. I cannot touch it. I can't be a part of it. My only option is to sit and wait for a lifeboat, a glimmer of freedom.

When that freedom comes, I grab life by the horns and ride for as long as possible. Until I'm shoved back into that small, locked room again. I know the room well; decorated its interior in black and reds. Sprayed it with cinnamon air freshener. But it doesn't feel like home. I'd like to burn the room down and never step foot inside again. That's not an option. I am the lioness, and it is my cage.

Baffling medical professionals for years, I have lived through a wild roller coaster of tests and specialists, searching high and low for answers. The answers were not what I expected, nor do I know how to live with them. Yet, they are still answers.

This is my truth, my journey, my experiences. Living undiagnosed is not something I would wish upon anyone. If you are one of these people, or know someone who is, you are not alone. There is a massive amount of people suffering with severe medical conditions which impact their quality of life. Some find answers over time, while others may never know the truth.

This is my truth.

Early Stages

As a teenager, there were random, bizarre symptoms which my doctor explained to me as "a part of growing up". Today, I know differently. Reaching towards 5'10" for a growing teenaged girl, it's considered normal to have dizzy spells, especially when standing up. There were periods of time when it would happen daily, and in my early twenties, my coworkers became concerned. One day always stands out for me. My office was in a tower, in the middle of a shop. I walked out the door towards the stairs and I collapsed on the landing. My vision was blurry and speckled as if I'd stared at a bright light for too long. Thankfully, a co-worker came up the stairs and helped me back into the office. If he hadn't shown up, I would have become more acquainted with that wooden staircase.

Little did I know it was all early symptoms of my condition.

After delivering my first child, things became strange. At first it was the extreme fatigue, which my spouse and I assumed was caused by low iron. After bringing my levels back up to normal, the fatigue never left. I'd collapsed a few times from dizziness or balance issues. It made life with a baby challenging. The most confusing change was the pressure buildup in my head, especially while changing elevation. Going up and down the stairs would cause major pressure headaches. Sometimes I thought my head would explode. I remember cursing that our shower was in the basement. Carrying a baby was difficult with that intense pressure in my head.

My family doctor decided to do a bit of digging. There was no explanation for the head pressure, and we were confused. Why would someone's head hurt while walking down the stairs? My blood pressure was on the low-normal side, ranging between 95/60 and 115/75. So, it was unrelated to a high blood pressure issue. What else could we look at? My head. After having two CT scans of my head, one in 2010 and another in 2011, they found nothing. We'd already done a stream of blood tests, and nothing jumped out. I had my blood sugar tolerance tested twice, where we ruled out diabetes. Everything else was normal. There was nothing else to look for.

Progression

Imagine sitting at the dinner table with family after a long workday. You're starving, but looking at your plate, something is missing, Ketchup. There it is, in the middle of the small round table. You reach for it, or try to, but it's like you're frozen in time. No matter how hard you try, you cannot get your arm to lift from the edge of the table. The harder you focus, the more distanced you feel. Across the table is your spouse.

Help! You're unable to speak.

A wave of numbness washes over you, from head down. You glare at your spouse, asking for help with your eyes. At last, they see you and rush to your side. Instincts takes over. They lay you on the floor and ask a series of questions.

"What's wrong? Are you in pain? Does your chest hurt? What's going on? Can you talk?"

They raise your feet, forcing blood to the upper half of your body, then roll you onto your side in case it's your heart.

After a few minutes of resting, your speech returns, but you are extremely weak. You explain the experience in hopes they can help you figure it out. They phone a relative who works in health care and may have ideas. Is it blood pressure? Is it a stroke? Is it MS? There's no way of knowing. You need sleep.

You want nothing more than to return to the kitchen table to eat with your family, but your body is not cooperating.

Thirty minutes of sleep helps you a bit, but everything feels off. It's a fight to sit up. For the rest of the evening, you lie on the couch, then move to your bed. Confused and frustrated, your mind is foggy. You feel drained and can't focus on anything. Until you recover, someone wraps your supper for later.

That is what I lived through.

This single moment in time sticks out amongst many others. Fear hit me hard then, as I'm sure it did for my future husband. Everything became more serious. These episodes snuck up from nowhere, hitting when least expected. Like visiting relatives or watching a show. At that time the episodes only happened once every six to eight weeks but became more frequent.

We followed the next probable course: checking for seizure activity. In the summer of 2011, my family doctor sent me for my first EEG, after which I was told there was no epileptic activity. This is something that bothers me. Years later, a family member suggested I build a binder filled with copies of all my medical records, including tests. When I read the report myself, of this EEG, it stated *contoured brain waves* which identified non-epileptic seizures, and I had *poor response to flashing light*. It also recommended going through a sleep deprived EEG.

No one told me about this aspect of the report. So many years have passed. Why didn't someone tell me? And why wasn't I sent for a sleep deprived EEG at that stage? I hold nothing against my doctor. He has been wonderful and thorough. I have a lot of respect for him. But it seems he overlooked some details in that report, which could have provided important answers. At that point, in 2011, I was unaware they confirmed seizure activity.

Next was the Holter monitor test, which was a small machine that recorded my heart activity. I carried it around everywhere I went and kept a log of what I was doing. Even when I was pooping. I don't think I put much effort into my log, as I recall apologizing to the medical team for the messy writing. If I could go back in time, I'd write things neater.

As expected, the test results came back clear, no sign of a heart problem.

Sleep Studies

For a full year, I did the best I could, living with these random episodes, as they became more and more frequent. I also suffered a miscarriage at three months along, on September 9, 2012. It was the most difficult period of my life. It took five weeks to replenish my iron levels and to return to work. Sometimes I wonder if this experience made my medical conditions worse, but I may never know for sure.

My fatigue became more pronounced, so my doctor lined me up for sleep studies. Not long after the miscarriage, still in 2012, I brought home a sleep recording machine. They are not the easiest things to sleep with. Yet the test cleared me of having any apnea and showed little evidence of snoring.

The following year, 2013, I attended a sleep lab for an overnight sleep study. It was very early into another pregnancy. This made the sleep study the most uncomfortable night ever. They did not build the bed for comfort and having so many wires attached to me was terrible. Morning sickness had me dry heaving in the bathroom, which, thankfully was located nearby.

I don't know how they got data during that endless night, because it felt as though I hadn't slept at all.

When I returned home, I was extremely thankful to be back in my own bed. It took time to get results, and when I went in, they confirmed I had no sleep disorders. The lady's kindness stays with me to this day. She said if no one helped me find answers, I should get in touch with her at the clinic and she'd help. It was very thoughtful of her to say, and it made me feel significant.

Today, when I read the report from the sleep study, the EKG identified abnormal heartbeats which disrupted normal rhythm. They called it "premature ventricular contractions". I still don't know what to do with this information. My doctor and I never discussed it. Was it important information? Do people often have premature ventricular contractions? I'm not sure, but at the rate my condition was progressing.

Exploring Seizures

In 2016, I was referred to a neurologist for the first time. At that stage, the seizure-like episodes had progressed to a point where I had tremors, muscle weakness, light sensitivity and more. They were also happening five out of seven days per week. During the rough weeks, it was daily. Going to work each day became more and more challenging. My workplace asked a lot of questions about how I was managing my illness and did I have plans to go on Disability.

The neurologist sent me for an MRI, and when I got the results, the details were a little vague. He told me there were no lesions, tumours or anything of major concern, except there was something about my brain protruding outside of my skull down into my spinal column area. He said there was no sign of crowding and no evidence it was causing my symptoms, and therefore no need for surgery. If I was thinking clearer then, I would have documented the name of this disorder he'd shared with me.

After explaining this to my family, we agreed I had an alien brain. Sure, it wasn't something I'd ever accuse anyone else of having, but there had to be some way to lighten the mood after learning about my deformed brain. Because I hadn't noted the name of the condition, we googled the information and just shook our heads. Everything I was experiencing was on the list of symptoms for a disorder called Chiari Malformation Type 1. Many patients with this disorder require decompression surgery, where doctors cut into the back of their heads and remove a section of bone to give the brain more space, and reduce pressure on their spinal chords. It was overwhelming to think about, and we trusted the neurologist. After a short while, I all but ignored what he'd said. The only thing that stuck was the reference to my alien brain.

We tried seizure medication, which made me feel so much worse. Then, we tried lorazepam which I took during an episode. It calmed things down, but then it forced me to remain in bed for two to three days after each dose. Then we tried anti-depressants, but I had digestive issues, so I couldn't take them for long. Overall, nothing helped. I still had no answers, no idea what it could be, no treatment and I felt... hopeless.

Meanwhile, I went through two more EEGs; the standard one like I'd had before, and a second for sleep deprivation. I cannot recall if these EEGs happened in 2017 or 2018. Memories from this time are foggy, but I know I had them. Both tests came back normal. I have tried to get a copy of these records to add to the medical binder, but my family doctor never received the reports.

In 2017, I had a second MRI and confirmed there'd been no changes. When things got rough, I saw the neurologist again, but all he could do was sign a doctor's note to give me time off work until I recovered from the rough patch. There was no direction and no plan to continue searching. After a while, I stopped seeing him as I felt we were not going anywhere.

Late that same year, my father had an accident. It was an unexpected event that shattered the bones in his leg, leading to amputation. While in the hospital waiting with my family for him to get out of surgery, I had multiple episodes. One nurse there witnessed an episode and asked what condition I had, to which my sisters explained I was undiagnosed. She suggested I request a referral to a different neurologist who ran a seizure clinic in the same hospital. Not long after, I made an appointment with my current neurologist and requested the referral to which he agreed to.

There was a bit of a wait but in early 2018 I stayed in the seizure clinic for 8 days, 7 nights. During this time, I was completely hooked up to electrodes, which were connected to the wall. They also videotaped the entire stay. Anytime I felt an episode coming on, I was to hit a specific button and nursing staff would rush in to take my blood pressure and monitor everything. I had two episodes per day that week. Family popped in to visit and giggled as they watched the neurological charts on the screen high on the wall. Every time I blinked my eyes, the lines would move, and it had me acting like a science experiment for my family's entertainment. At one point, I used the bathroom only to hear everyone in the room laughing so hard while I intentionally blinked repeatedly, which increased the activity on the screen. At least I can take a small positive memory from the experience.

In the middle of my first night, I awoke to find someone staring at me. At the end of my bed, every night, a staff member would sit in a chair and watch me. It was really creepy. But I remember one night there was a kind lady there, and we sat up for about an hour just talking. It made me feel a lot less like an experiment and more like a real person.

Three months passed before I received my results. The conversation I had with the specialist stands out clearly in my mind today. It was like a huge emotional tidal wave. First, he said I did not have epilepsy. Second, he said there were spikes on my neurological charts so he could guarantee me the episodes were real. Third, he said it's possible I've experienced something very emotional in my life which is causing these episodes and I needed to be referred to a different specialist. This time, a neurological psychologist.

What a lot to take in. It was a relief that I did not have epilepsy, as I knew that could mean losing my license and possibly my job. Getting the confirmation that I was not imagining things, and I wasn't going crazy, was something I needed to hear, and something that I repeated to other people in my life who I wasn't confident believed what I was experiencing. But the last part really hit me hard.

Emotional trauma may have caused my seizures.

Did that mean I'm emotionally traumatized? Was there something wrong with me mentally? How could I even explore what could have caused such damage? At that moment, I cried. Tears streamed down my cheeks as I tried to accept his words. How could I move on from this? A neurological psychologist? I'd never heard of this before.

The epileptic neurologist told me there was a waiting list. It could be one year, or two, before being contacted for an appointment. A part of me thought, there's no way this neuro psychologist could help me. I'm not emotionally traumatized. The other part of me wondered if there was some aspect of truth. Yes, I'd been through a few things, which I will go over in the "Emotional Trauma" section of this book. I just didn't feel it had as much of an impact on me as they were implying.

Surviving

While I was waiting for this appointment, I had to fight to survive. I had to learn what I was capable of and not capable of. What were my triggers?

Mowing the lawn was an issue. I could do a few rows, but then my body would give up and I'd have to stop and lie on the ground, waiting for help to get up or waiting to recover. I never did it alone, and always had my partner with me.

Riding a bicycle used to be easy, but as the years went by, it became next to impossible. I'd get on, go around the block without an issue, but as soon as I got back into the driveway, I struggled to get off. I couldn't even walk into my house without help.

Let's talk about housework. Emptying the dishwasher? Episode. Bending down to change the laundry? Episode. Sweeping the floor, washing the floor, or vacuuming? Episode. There's only so much I could put on my partner. He has been my rock through this entire process. If I was in the middle of making supper and froze in place, or lost my balance, he'd be there in a heartbeat, helping me to bed and taking over the cooking. Many nights, I was incapable of tucking the kids into bed. Sometimes I'd think I was doing well, and I'd go to a writing meeting five minutes away, but then I'd have an episode and not be able to drive myself home.

Some days I felt like giving up. I couldn't stay on top of the housework and some people who came into our home would make rude remarks. They didn't understand. I tried not to hold it against them, but it hurt. There were episodes that were so bad that I felt terrible that my kids had to witness it. I can't imagine how my husband felt, carrying our entire world on his back, taking care of me, the kids, the house. It's a lot for anyone to handle on their own. But I just couldn't do it.

The guilt that weighed on me was monstrous. I was always hard on myself. Why couldn't I keep up? Why couldn't I keep the house clean and cook for my family? Why was it so damn hard to go to work every day?

What was wrong with me?

Emotional Trauma

Please take this as a trigger warning. I will not get into gruesome details, but if you are sensitive to life events, please skip this section entirely.

To be clear, I do not blame anyone in my family for these events, as no one was aware they were going on. As a young girl, there were a handful of times where I experienced sexual harassment. The first time, a friend of the family had been over with their boys. One boy was trying to pressure me into kissing him while hiding in a ditch during hide and seek. Thankfully, I was smart enough to run away and nothing happened. But years later, his younger brother had more luck.

A group of us were watching movies in the basement of our home. All the lights were off, and their eyes focused on the television. I think I was about 11 years old. I was sitting in a chair with a blanket draped over me, when that younger brother propped a chair next to me and threw a blanket over himself. He slipped his hands into my blanket and started touching me. All over. Even in my pants. I was so scared, as no one had touched me like that before and all I wanted to do was scream. Instead, I froze in place and said nothing. Eventually they left, and I didn't tell anyone what had happened. Being older now, looking back at it all, the only thing that sticks out to me is that terrible feeling of being trapped and everyone else's eyes being glued to the TV while I needed help. It was like living in a creepy movie, the kind that sends chills down your spine. No, I don't blame them, and I never did. But that fear, and the expressions on everyone's face in the blue-white glow from the TV, has stuck with me.

One summer, our family went to an outdoor concert in the evening. It was a regular event where we lived. Famous performers would sing on stage, then there were fireworks and a light show with sailboats. I was walking down the street with my older sister and step-siblings when I felt something jab between my legs and backside. It took me a moment to realize it was a man's hand. I turned around to see a tall biker man laughing like they do in creepy movies, towering over me, all proud of himself. As he continued to laugh, he turned and walked away to brag about it to his buddies. My siblings rushed me back to our parents, where they called the police. I had to sit in a cruiser and give a statement to an officer who was not very good at talking to people my age. My memories were instantly foggy, and describing the man was very difficult. I'd told the officer the man was wearing a hat, but I know that wasn't true. It was like my brain had clouded the image of him to protect itself. But I remember what he looks like now.

One period is hard to write about, and it involves someone who was active in my life. I cannot explain who this person was, out of respect for the people involved, but I can tell you this person was emotionally abusive. They'd plant seeds in my mind and trick me into talking about things they wanted to hear. Then they would spin my words and try to play people against each other. This person would yell and freak out for reasons that made no sense to me, leaving me walking on eggshells anytime they were around. Some moments were good and even fun. But then it would confuse me when they'd completely flip into a different personality. All I can say beyond this was that it was throughout my teenage years, and it took a long time to recover from this. I'm not sure if I ever truly recovered from the emotional abuse I suffered.

When I was 18 years old, before I met my current husband, I was raped. It was someone I'd met a few times, someone who'd passed by where I worked in a clothing store in the mall. One weekend, there was a house party, and I was with my best friend. That guy was there, too. I'd had a crush on him, and I knew he liked me, or at least I hoped he did. He was tall with blond hair and blue eyes, a little muscular. Nice looking guy. After a few drinks, we went to the basement to make out. At that point in life, I'd only been with one person, the one I'd lost my virginity with. So, I had no intention of sleeping with a guy I'd only just started seeing. Things were moving fast, and

I rolled away, still fully clothed. I think. I may have been topless, things are foggy.

He hinted he wanted to keep going, and I said no, I'm not experienced, I've only done it once. Well, he got on and did what he wanted anyway, while I lay there like a statue, afraid and unable to move. Once he finished, he slept like nothing had happened. That night I had to lie beside the man who forced me to sleep with him, pretending everything was okay. I'm not even sure I really slept. I was too afraid to say anything to anyone the next day. I never told my parents, not until I was older. Months later, I found out he was spreading rumours about me, saying I was the worst he'd ever slept with, and it was a massive mistake.

In my adult years, I ran into him again at a social. He wanted to buy me a drink, but I said no thanks. Then he apologized for what had happened when we were younger. I don't think he realized what he'd done, and so I just said thanks and walked away. It didn't really help me get over it, but maybe to move past it. I felt bad for him. I'd been told he had become addicted to drugs. He was thin, pale, and looked twice his age. The image of him in my mind from that night, when I was eighteen, was not the image I saw before me. It was like that guy no longer existed.

In 2012, after my episodes had started, we suffered a terrible loss. We had one child already and I was pregnant with our second. One week away from our three-month ultrasound, I started spotting. We went into the hospital where they told me to go home and rest, to reduce the risk of miscarriage, although so far things looked okay. The next day, I woke up in excruciating pain and more blood. We went to the emergency department again, where I sat at the front entrance screaming in pain while the staff argued about why someone hadn't sent me through yet.

That day, I lost my baby. It didn't stop there. I continued bleeding, in pain, with no end in sight. They transported me by ambulance to another hospital. It was a rough ride. When we got there, I waited on a stretcher in the hallway. When I went numb the paramedic who was watching me tilted the bed so that the blood would go to my head, reducing my risk of losing consciousness. From there, they rushed me into an operating room, where they proceeded with a D&C. If you aren't sure what that is, basically they had to go inside and scrape the lining of my uterus to clean out anything remaining, telling my body that there was nothing left to push out.

It took five weeks to get my iron levels back to where they should be, and to get to a point where I could stay out of bed for any length of time. Telling my first born was one of the hardest things to do. He was three years old, and we'd told him I was pregnant. He knew the baby was in there. Then one day it wasn't. My sister had taken him for a few days to give us time to accept what had happened. When she brought him home, one of the first things our son said was, "Are you sad, mommy? The baby is dead?" He kept asking questions. He meant well, but it's hard to remain strong when someone says those words to you point blank.

Returning to work was stressful. People looked at me like I was emotionally scarred and unable to do anything. All I wanted was to move forward and keep focused on my job. I know they meant well and wanted to be there for me. It was hard meeting a co-worker's new baby months later. We were pregnant at the same time, and our kids would have been the same age.

Shopping in a store caused panic attacks. Being in crowds made me anxious. I felt like I was falling apart. Looking for emotional stability, I went to counselling. She gave me tips on how to manage panic attacks. Grounding methods. It helped but I'm still not great at shopping in crowded stores.

It took a long time for me to be capable of looking at another baby, even on TV. Yet, in 2013, we conceived again. This time the pregnancy was successful, and we were blessed with our second 10-pound baby boy. Yes, both our boys were 10 pounds at birth. It was like giving birth to 3-month-old babies.

Every Spring, I plant at least one white flower in my garden. While I do, I think of the unborn child that we lost, and imagine their smiling face. Each time I water the white flower, it's like I'm parenting the child we never got to meet.

There were more events beyond this, but these are the ones that stick out the most. I can relive them at anytime, which brings back an emotional intensity. Fear. Sadness. Loss. Anxiety. Panic. Although it all still haunts me today, it also strengthened me.

Life Continues

Although coping with my medical condition wasn't easy, life has continued. We have two beautiful boys who were ten pounds each at birth. Hockey has become a huge part of our lifestyle. The oldest is a very talented goalie and the youngest has a natural skill on skates. Although I miss many ice times, I attend as many practices and games as my body will allow. I am a very proud Hockey Mom.

My partner and I have been together since 2001 and were engaged Christmas of 2006. In 2018 we were married at a beautiful barn which had been rebuilt after a devastating fire. It was the perfect day with our two boys by our sides; a day filled with family and close friends, food and dancing. Leading up to that day my biggest fear was having an episode walking down the aisle. Thankfully, I managed to make it through the entire ceremony without any issues. It was a lot of work planning such a special day, but I had a lot of family close by to help, and I've never been happier.

Checking for Sugar and Blood Pressure Issues

In 2019, my husband had noticed a difference in how I felt after eating meals. It was very common for me to have an episode after supper each night. Sometimes, he would raise my legs in the air and hold them, which would bring me out of the episode faster. We had done sugar tolerance tests twice and nothing ever came of it.

After explaining this event to my doctor, he suggested I do a food diary and get a blood sugar tester for home. From there, he connected with a dietitian to review my log. I would test my blood sugar before eating, right after eating, an hour after eating, and so on. The dietitian reviewed everything and said I process my sugars very well and I in no way have a blood sugar problem.

My family doctor checked my blood pressure, and it was at a healthy low. He suggested getting a blood pressure machine for home so that I could document my blood pressure randomly. After keeping a log for that, with random checking, there was no evidence of a blood pressure issue.

Discovering Omega-3

Exhaustion overwhelmed me most days, and I had little energy. Yet, once in a while, there would be a good day. A day where I had energy, remained positive and could keep up with my family. In late 2019, we noticed that these days often coincided with days we ate fish. Pickerel. Eating pickerel lead to anywhere from one to three good days. But what was in fish that could give me that boost?

After researching what nutrients each type of fish contained on the internet, the only thing we came up with was omega-3. If you look up omega-3 on the internet it talks about how it safeguards your neuropathy and seizure patients often take it as part of their health regiment. What harm could taking a supplement do?

It started with one pill daily. After a month, we noticed a clarity of mind. So, we increased it to 2 pills, then 3. Eventually I researched how much was safe to take, which took me to a maximum dose of 6 pills, or 2 pills three times per day with meals. This totaled 6,000 mg of fish oil per day.

How did I feel? Like a million bucks! Yes, I still had rough patches, but at one point I got down to one episode every two weeks. It felt like a miracle. How could fish oil make me feel so good? Yes, I had to be careful and only do one active thing per day, but I was surviving. Taking it easy but living a little more. Still, if I did too much, I'd end up going through a rough patch again. The worst days were during the week prior to my monthly cycle. I had more frequent episodes, and often worse than my usual. I still couldn't ride a bicycle, or do much cleaning, but I could stay mobile mostly.

My brain fog faded. I could accomplish more at work. My mood had improved, and I could go out a bit more. It wasn't an answer or a treatment a doctor would recommend, but our discovery helped me get through the tough times. When I shared this news with my doctor, he was fully supportive of staying on omega-3 fish oil long term. I also got the approval from a dietitian. One day I took a chance and went to 7 pills, but my eyelids twitched for days! Never again. 6 pills were the maximum safe amount I could tolerate

Although we'd found something to help, the thought of not having a diagnosis weighed heavily on my mind. Why couldn't anyone figure out what was wrong with me? How could omega-3 make such an improvement on my condition?

Exploring Other Options

Having no further direction from my doctor, which I did not blame him for, I felt lost and depressed. How could I get better and improve my quality of life without answers and guidance? I wasn't ready to give up searching. Why would I? I had a loving family, including two boys and a very supportive husband. I had a career in manufacturing and the potential to keep pushing forward with my writing and self-publishing. So, I considered other healthcare options.

I'd heard many people had gone to a Naturopathic doctor. I wasn't sure if it was right for me. But what did I have to lose? I found one of the top-rated naturopathic facilities in Manitoba and contacted them for an appointment. Yet when I explained over the phone that I had a neurological condition, they recommended I first meet with their Neurological Chiropractor. To this I said, "What is that?" I'd never heard of this before. Apparently, this is a licenced chiropractor who specializes in the neurological system. This gives the individual a unique perspective and understanding of how the neural pathways connect to your body. So, I said, "sure, why not?"

Upon first meeting this man, he impressed me. He was extremely thorough and paid special attention to how I was feeling. Hearing I had Chiari Malformation, he also paid for a disc that housed my MRI images. After reviewing the MRI, he also allowed me to borrow the disc to get an excellent view of what my brain looks like. Let me tell you, it was very interesting. Especially when you compare it to a "normal" brain image.

After a few appointments, he had me convinced that my episodes were happening when I looked up. Once we figured this out, I could bring on an episode by command, anytime I looked up! Yet it also caused a lot of panic. I began wearing a baseball cap everywhere I went, as a reminder to not look upwards beyond the visor. At work, I kept a little sunhat in my desk drawer in case I ever needed to block out the light, or in case I forgot to avoid looking up. I remember shopping for this sunhat with a group of ladies from work. We met at the dollar store close to my home, and we all went crazy buying lots of things. I also picked up an extendable metal back scratcher to keep in my desk, which I have to this day. Sitting at work with that black, topless sunhat, everyone teased me. I looked like a card dealer from a casino.

Back to the medical stuff.

When my episodes were bad, the neurological chiropractor said my brain was taking in too much information and it would be a good idea to wear sunglasses, reduce screen brightness, and wear the hat to reduce the impact of neon lights at work. Whenever I hit a rough patch, I follow this advice and it almost always helps me get through the day.

Whenever I went to see him, he gave me instructions for neurological exercises to complete at home. Although I followed this as best I could, I never really understood it nor received validation that it was helping me. I'm sure it was, but I just didn't feel any difference. After a while, I reduced the frequency of my appointments. Once the pandemic hit in 2020, I stopped going altogether. At first it was because they'd temporarily closed, but then I accepted it wasn't improving anything for me.

Finding a Gluten Issue

While surviving this odd undiagnosed medical condition, I also experienced digestive issues. Previously, I was diagnosed with IBS (Irritable Bowel Syndrome) and Acid Reflux, but sometimes after supper, my stomach would become so bloated that my skin pulled tight, and it physically hurt. I also had major abdominal cramps off and on, which were gas pains. Having met a co-worker with Celiac disease, I wondered if I had the same thing.

My doctor had no problem sending me for a simple blood test, and when the results came in, he sounded quite shocked on the phone. A person without a gluten issue would have a specific test result, which I honestly cannot remember the name of, but the number should be no higher than 15 or 20. My number was 216! It was extremely clear I had a gluten issue, but in order to confirm medically, I needed to go for a biopsy. In June 2020 I went for a stomach biopsy where they confirmed I had Celiac disease. The instant I was out of the procedure, they told me to start a gluten-free diet.

If you haven't heard of celiac disease before, it's where every time you ingest gluten, it causes damage to your intestines. Sometimes you feel symptoms, other times nothing, but the damage still occurs.

Leaving this untreated can increase your risk of developing other medical conditions and cause neurological damage, which could also lead to seizures. Today I still wonder if I have neurological damage from this disease.

It was a difficult diet change! Learning to read the labels was a nightmare, but after a while I got the hang of it. Cutting out some of my favourite chocolate bars was probably the most difficult. And the Icelandic Cake at Christmas? Really? And if I wanted to make gluten-free pancakes, *I* had to make a batch that only I would eat. Some gluten-free bread-type products are extremely dry, so after a while I stopped eating much of it and stuck with healthier options.

What changes did I see? The biggest was that I lost fifteen pounds in a matter of 8 months. That was just cutting out gluten items and not really dieting, so to speak. Then, after about 10 months, I noticed my legs were thinner and so was my face. It was like my body had been in a constant state of inflammation when I ate gluten. The bloating almost completely stopped after meals, and it was rare to get gas pains. It was a massive improvement on my overall health.

But it didn't stop the episodes.

Writing With Medical Conditions

One coping method I have enjoyed over the years is writing. Sitting in a quiet space with no distractions and disappearing into a fictional world allowed me some aspect of escape from my tough reality. I started writing after my first son was born, and I have not stopped. I've been writing for as long as I've been living with these medical conditions.

As my health conditions have progressed, it has become more and more difficult to continue writing. With light sensitivity, looking at the screen for long periods of time reduces my productivity. It's been frustrating leaving many projects incomplete. Yet I've pushed forward.

In 2020, I began my self-publishing journey. I took one story I'd written a few years prior, called Red Leaves, and I turned it into an eBook. That lead me to write more stories in the same series which were all published as eBooks, and each story displays how I grew as a writer. Every story in the collection became better than the previous. The only thing that slowed me down was not being able to look at the computer screen for long writing sessions.

One of my other writing friends recommended joining the "AuthorTube" community, who are a large group of writers across the world who maintain their own YouTube channels dedicated to writing and publishing. I knew taking on more was not the best idea, but I couldn't help myself. I learned how to record, edit, and upload videos about writing. I called it "Tania's Writing Realm". But doing this led to increasing the frequency of my episodes.

Video editing requires a lot of time and focus, all of it staring at movement on a screen. Although I enjoyed the feeling of releasing videos, each of them has caused symptoms. Have I stopped recording and releasing videos? No. I'm stubborn. I still want to live my life to the fullest and if that means releasing video content, so be it. I don't want to be held back and I don't want to give up my writing or YouTube channel.

Looking to grow my audience, I also started a podcast with the same name as my YouTube channel. The benefit of using the podcast host service I selected is that it also uploads each episode as a static video with audio directly to my channel. This has helped me reduce time with video editing, because instead of doing one video each week, I release one video bi-weekly and the podcast episode in between. This has been a tremendous help, and I may lean more into the podcast instead of the YouTube channel in the future. Without this podcast, I may have considered giving up on my channel.

To me, giving up means that I have failed. It means not being fulfilled in life. It means that I'm not capable of accomplishing my dreams. Giving up is not an option.

Returning to the Naturopath Option

By this point, I had gone through so many medical tests and specialists. I'd gotten a few answers and ruled out so many other possible diagnoses, but I still didn't have any direction. Instead of sitting around doing nothing about it, I returned to the idea of seeing a naturopath. Speaking with the same facility as before, they referred me to a different building across the city where the top-rated naturopath was located.

Times had changed. No longer were most medical appointments in person. Instead, most facilities requested phone or video appointments, if possible, to reduce the risk of spreading the "C" word. Over the phone, I met with the naturopath. The very first place he went to with my condition was checking for heavy metals poisoning. It was not something ever discussed with my family doctor and it's not something I would have thought to ask about.

Although I had to pay for everything out of my pocket, I went along with the test he recommended. Guess what I had to do. I bet you can't! I had to take home ten large pills, take them all at once, which was not fun, then I had to bag and refrigerate my pee in my fridge for a period of about six hours. That's right,

I kept my pee in my fridge, and I prayed my kids wouldn't try to open the bag. Then I had to shake the plastic bag, pour a small amount into a specimen container and... are you ready for it? I had to mail my pee across the border to a lab. That's not even the funny part. Because I worked business hours, the only way I could send it out was to bring my package of pee to work.

Have I mentioned I work in a metal shop? Thankfully, I have a close friend who worked in shipping. I'd passed the package along to her and she scheduled the courier to pick it up. Only she'd placed it on a table outside of the shipping office. Guess what happened. Someone placed a metal part on top of my pee container! When I saw it, I completely freaked out. If that container broke, my pee would go everywhere! Then I'd have to go through the entire process, of taking 10 large pills and bagging my pee again. Thankfully, after inspecting the package, it appeared undamaged, and I asked my friend to babysit my pee a little better.

After a couple of weeks, I received a call to book another appointment with the naturopath. When the appointment came, the naturopath said I had high heavy metals toxicity. There was no way to identify where it came from, even after talking to my parents, husband, and workplace. My workplace did not use these metals, and it was very odd to find such high levels.

Next came the detox. Two rounds. That is 18 weeks of heavy pills, vitamins, and special supplements. Then I had to do yet another pee-bagging test. After which, there was a minor change in my heavy metal levels which made me wonder if it was a waste of time.

How did I feel after all that? The only change I noticed was that memories were resurfacing from my childhood. Not bad ones, though. Most of them sweet. Then I started dreaming more at night. Aside from that, there was no impact on my episodes or level of fatigue.

After this, the naturopathic doctor switched his focus to diet. He asked that I cut back on carbs and eat healthier. This is when I started noticing a bigger difference in my energy levels. What food could have been causing such a big change? Either way, he asked me to continue with low carb eating, as it was making a difference.

Although this wonderful doctor had a lot of great ideas to improve my overall health, the cost was too much for what we were getting out of it, so we decided it was time to stop seeing him. If I had a money tree out back, I would have kept going through all the steps he'd suggested. But it just wasn't being realistic. What *was* important was discovering what was causing these seizure-like events and the extreme fatigue, then managing it.

Discovering my Diagnosis

Whenever I had a full meal, I noticed a huge lull in my energy levels. This had come up in 2019, which led to blood sugar testing. Yet I had a sneaky suspicion it had something to do with blood pressure. So, much like the first blood pressure log, I took it upon myself to record another one, but focusing on meals like I had done with sugar.

This is where things got interesting.

Before eating, my blood pressure ranged from 116/78 to 110/73. About twenty minutes after eating, it would drop to 105/70 to 100/60 range. I experienced numbness, weakness, slurred or loss of speech, and occasionally mild tremors. It would become difficult to hold my head upright, and my vision was not quite right.

Boom! I'd found another answer on my own. Googling it on the internet, we researched a condition called Postprandial Hypotension, which is basically a blood pressure drop off up to 20 points on the top or bottom number while digesting food. This happens when your body pools blood in your digestive system in order to process foods. For people who have this condition, their bodies work harder to digest food, which causes blood pressure to drop. My blood was leaving my brain in order to help me process food. Wow! Who would have thought?

From there, I brought my log to my next doctor's appointment. It surprised him. I think he felt bad that he hadn't picked up on this before, but he confirmed the diagnosis. In addition, he asked me to sit and take another BP reading, then stand and take a second reading. Boom! Another diagnosis. Orthostatic Hypotension, which is where blood pressure drops by 20 points on either number when changing position. This explained why I had such a hard time cleaning or doing much physical movement in life. It also explains why in my younger years, I was experiencing dizzy spells and feeling off upon standing. And why I've always had a tough time cleaning or remaining active.

On the bright side, there was medication. Right away he prescribed me Florinef, which is a steroid intended to reduce the intense blood pressure drop after changing position. After a couple of weeks of taking it, I noticed a big difference. The only downside was it didn't help with the Postprandial Hypotension.

Learning about my new conditions, I did more research on omega-3, and learned that it can lower your blood pressure. I stopped taking it, which my doctor supported. At first, I was unsure if it was the right move, but the new medication was helping so much that I didn't really notice a difference. At least, not at first.

It ended up being a trade-off. Florinef helped with my orthostatic symptoms but did nothing for the blood pressure drops after eating full meals. My activities became easier between meals, but anytime I ate something filling or heavy, I suffered a setback. After struggling with this for two months, I started adding omega-3 back into my daily routine, along with vitamin D3. I had been taking D3 before the heavy metals' roller coaster, but I'd gone off because of the number of other supplements I was taking.

To start, I took just one omega-3 pill, instead of the six that I used to take, and after two weeks, I noticed another big difference. Although I still experienced the blood pressure drops after eating, it reduced the symptoms during that drop. Instead, I'd feel sleepy and lazy, which was much better than having a seizure-like episode.

After discovering the effects omega-3 had on the Postprandial Hypotension, I let my doctor know I was taking it again but in a lower dose. He fully supported my decision. The combination of the supplements and the Florinef made a tremendous impact on my quality of life. Unfortunately, taking these two pieces out of the equation, or at least reducing the extremity of the episodes, revealed there was still something neurological going on. Light sensitivity and seizures still occurred outside of the blood pressure drops. They felt a little different from those events. There were more tremors, and it looked more like a typical seizure. Yet I knew they were non epileptic, so what could cause them?

The Final Pieces

In 2021, after over 3 years of waiting, I finally got the appointment I'd been waiting for with the neurological psychologist. It still felt like I was being sent to this specialist only because no one else could help me. Yet I still held a glimmer of hope in my heart, because after ruling out so much and being diagnosed with so many things, it made other issues more apparent.

During the three years, off and on, I'd wondered about this specialist and how easily she would be to work with. Would she be understanding and patient? Would she be quick to assume I had some emotional issues that were causing my episodes, without doing any kind of examination? A few times, I visited a website online where doctors had reviews from previous patients, including a star rating. Hers had a mix of reviews. Some were very pleasant and positive, while a few were unhappy with their experience. It left me feeling uncertain and less than confident that I'd find answers.

Because of the pandemic, this appointment was a video call. When she came on the screen and smiled at me, that feeling of uncertainty melted away. She was warm, friendly, and didn't seem to have an ounce of negativity or urge to rush me through our discussion. After asking me a lot of questions, she wanted more information about the episodes that were not related to the blood pressure drops. Putting everything into words helped me analyze things myself.

Light sensitivity came up first, for which she suggested going to an optometrist to request blue filter glasses. Her opinion was that it was from me working on a computer for so many years, as well as writing on the side. It's very common for people to experience this light sensitivity when working in a desk job.

During meetings with co-workers, my heart would race and have palpitations. Sometimes, I'd be short of breath and experience mild numbness in my limbs. There were moments I'd space out completely with difficulty focusing and my speech became slow. In this scenario, the specialist said it was the exact description of severe anxiety. To confirm she asked me a series of questions, to which I admitted to her, and myself, that I worried a lot. I was an over thinker who imagined every scenario and outcome in a matter of seconds. For this she recommended I consider medication. She listed three options plus one supplement if I preferred no medication.

Honestly, I've always known that I worry too much and over-think, but I hadn't realized that it was serious enough to cause medical symptoms. At night when I get up to use the bathroom, I can rarely fall right back to sleep. My mind kicks into high gear and my thoughts swirl in circles like a funnel cloud, starting tremendous gusts of emotion that overwhelm me. The thoughts could be memories or an unending movie playing about possible events that could happen based on certain actions. Falling back to sleep only works if I recognize the tornado and take deep breaths, avoiding thoughts, and forcing my body to relax one limb at a time.

The next episode I explained to the specialist was the more seizure-like event, caused by bright lights, too much eye movement, looking around too much, or playing fast-paced video game. Because a previous neurologist had ruled out epilepsy, and apparently confirmed a non-epileptic seizure which I hadn't realized, this specialist's opinion was that I have a condition called Functional Neurological Disorder, or "FND". This is where messages are not being passed through the brain accurately. Scientists and specialists have not confirmed the cause of this condition, however, there is some evidence emotional trauma could be the trigger. Another way of explaining it is the psychological area of my brain is hi-jacking the mobility section.

There were events in my life that may have caused this condition, but it is impossible for me to pinpoint it myself. When I talked to my family about everything, they suggested I go to a therapist. I'd been to counsellors throughout elementary school, high school and occasionally in my adult life. Yes, it helped a lot, but I wasn't sure how a full-blown therapist could help with the physical symptoms.

The first few days after hearing my final diagnosis, I felt depressed. No one wants to hear they have a medical condition for which no specific cause has been identified, with no cure or treatment available, and that could one day leave them on Disability. Does this mean I'll be living like this for the rest of my life? Will I never reach a point in time where I feel 100%

normal and strong? Is my doctor going to take away my driver's licence and tell me to go on Disability? These questions burned in my head, day after day.

Two weeks after the virtual appointment, I met with my family doctor in person to discuss the results. The letter from the Neuro Psychologist stated I had previously been diagnosed with PNES by the Epileptic Neurologist in 2018. This is Psychogenic Non-Epileptic Seizures. Another diagnosis I was unaware of. The doctor prescribed me medication to reduce the severe anxiety, which over time may reduce these episodes. He also confirmed that I should continue working for as long as I can, as I have already managed to continue working all these years.

Going on Disability is not something I'm ready to do. It can cause depression and make my conditions worse. Here is the full list of diagnosis, including the small ones:

1. Acid Reflux
2. IBS (a possible misdiagnosis)
3. Celiac Disease
4. Chiari Malformation Type 1
5. Orthostatic Hypotension
6. Postprandial Hypotension
7. Severe Anxiety
8. Psychogenic Non-Epileptic Seizures (PNES)
9. Functional Neurological Disorder (FND)

Number nine sticks out like a sore thumb. The last six are the causes of my seizure-like episodes, each of them similar to the other, yet different. What do I do with all of this?

I survive.

It has been at least twenty years since the first symptoms started. It has been thirteen years since things kicked into high gear and we began our search. Today, as I write this, it has been three weeks since I received my final diagnosis.

Finally, after living undiagnosed for so long, I have answers. What did it take? A loving, supportive husband at my side, for whom I'll be forever thankful. Two boys who love their mother, no matter what she goes through or how she looks during the episodes. A workplace and its employees, like a second family, with patience and understanding that never ended. My best friend at work who rushes through the building at moments notice to support me. Other family members trying their best to be supportive, even if they aren't there at my side. Close writing friends who encourage me and show compassion through my difficult times.

It takes strength and willpower to get out of bed every day without giving up, regardless of how many times I felt like staying there.

Although I may never find the cause of these diagnosis, at least now I can move forward.

Now, I can begin my next journey: Healing.

About the Author

While struggling with an undiagnosed medical condition, Tania Stephanson has been tucked away honing her writing skills as a member of the Interlake Writer's Guild in Manitoba, Canada. She has multiple publications in the Lake Winnipeg Writer's Group's (LWWG) bi-annual release of their anthology *Voices*, as well as a breastfeeding article with Parent's Canada and a Parmesan Chicken recipe in *Tomato Slices.* In 2020, amid the chaos of the pandemic, Tania ventured into the self-publishing world. To support other writers and authors, she also runs a YouTube channel called "Tania's Writing Realm" which soon will be the name of her very first podcast. Other publications may be found under the author names T.S. Stephanson.

Medical Definitions

What is it?

In my words...

Acid Reflux – stomach acid that flows backwards into your esophagus. This is made worse by eating greasy or acidic food, or even over-eating.

Irritable bowel Syndrome (IBS) – a chronic condition that causes cramping, abdominal pain, bloating, gas, and bowel issues (constipation or diarrhea). This can be made worse by eating certain foods.

Celiac Disease – eating gluten causes an immune response in the small intestine. Many believe this can cause damage to your intestines and potentially other organs in your body. If left untreated for a long time, it can also cause neurological damage.

Chiari Malformation Type 1 – the cerebellum (a section of your brain) is deformed, displacing the lower section (tonsils) into the spinal canal. This also puts additional pressure on the brain. Some patients are often left with severe headaches, which *may* only be improved by surgery.

Orthostatic Hypotension – blood pressure suddenly reduces by changing position, most commonly when standing from sitting or lying down.

Postprandial Hypotension – After eating, blood rushes to your digestive system which in turn causes a drastic drop in blood pressure. This response most often occurs after eating a carb heavy meal or eating too much in general.

Severe Anxiety – an extreme reaction to stress, which includes feeling nervous or anxious. This can reduce your ability to function normally in life.

Psychogenic Non-Epileptic Seizures (PNES) – a type of seizure that does not have any known physical causes. It is believed these are developed by people who have a stressful life, mental illness, or have suffered emotional trauma.

Functional Neurological Disorder (FND) – the brain does not function normally. This may be connected to extreme stress and emotional trauma. Not everything is known about this disorder.

Other Publications

<u>Author Name: Tania Stephanson</u>

Crime Thrillers

(Lighter Reads)

Red Leaves

Red Snow

Red Lies

Red River

Red Secrets

Red Crime Thriller Collection (includes above)

Non Fiction

Life Beats

Nerdalific's AutoBudget

A Recipe in *Tomato Slices*

Breast Feeding Article on *Parents Canada* Website

Author Names: Tania Simcock and Tania Stephanson

Multiple publications available in the Lake Winnipeg Writer's Group's journal called *Voices*. This includes short stories and poetry.

Author Name: T.S. Stephanson

High Fantasy

Tales of Elganthis: Volume 1

More titles to come in Tania's High Fantasy world of *Elganthis*

Media Links

Facebook Page:

https://www.facebook.com/TaniaStephanson

Author Website:

https://www.taniastephanson.ca/

Writing/Author YouTube Channel "Tania's Writing Realm"

https://www.youtube.com/channel/UCeQfXZ5TmkwznxdqcJFRzrg

Nerdalific YouTube Channel (Software Tutorials):

https://www.youtube.com/channel/UCq3En_I6uMUhtaFGUpCyJ-w

Find Tania's eBooks:

Amazon Kindle

Apple Books

Barnes & Noble

Raokuten kobo

Scribd

Tolino

OverDrive

Bibliotheca

Baker & Taylor

Vivlio

Library Direct

cloudLibrary

Gardners Extended Retail

Odilo

Gardners Library

Smashwords

Are You A Writer?

Watch Tania on her YouTube channel to learn more about the art of being a Self-Published / Indie Author.

Listen to Tania's podcast for great quotes, writing contest details, creativity prompts and more!

Find her writing chat group on Facebook.

All are entitled **"Tania's Writing Realm"**.

Message to Readers

Thank you for taking the time to purchase and read this book. If you are living without a full diagnosis, or know someone who is, remember that you are NOT alone. Many people across the world survive one day at a time, hoping and praying for answers that will help them discover ways to improve their lifestyles.

Never give up.

From Tania